# How to Start a Mobile Spa

## Make Money by Helping Other People Relax

Isabella Yearwood

By reading this notice, the reader agrees that under no circumstances is the author responsible for any losses, direct or indirect, that are incurred as a result of the use of information contained within this book, including, but not limited to, errors, omissions, or inaccuracies.

# Table of Contents

# Introduction

There's nothing else quite like a spa day! People love being pampered! And people are also living stressful and busy lives.

They need to incorporate self-care and a spa day is a perfect way to be able to do that. You come in and make people feel relaxed and you're going to get paid to do it! You can't just start your business and expect people to magically call you.

You're going to have to put in some work to be successful. My aim with this book is to help walk you through what you need to do to run a successful mobile spa.

# Chapter 1: Why This Business Makes Sense Being Mobile

There's no doubt that spas are successful. The reasons for this are because of what I mentioned in the introduction. People want to be pampered.

They want to be relaxed. They need to reduce their stress from their strenuous job or personal life. The list of reasons goes on and on. Yes, a brick-and-mortar spa can definitely have success, but it's easier to get started with a mobile spa and it's going to provide you with some unique benefits that a physical location can't offer you.

## Fewer Overhead Costs

The biggest expense you're going to incur with a physical location is the lease for your spa. You have to have a location to operate out of and this is easily going to cost you thousands of dollars per month. Not to mention you could be locked into a multi-year lease, which could make it more challenging to expand or move your business.

With a mobile spa, you get to avoid the major cost of leasing a space for your business. It's going to be far easier to start a mobile spa due to the lower amount of overhead costs.

This is great if you don't have a lot of spare capital to invest to get things going. You can keep your upfront costs to a minimum and get straight to servicing clients so you can start making money.

## More Flexibility

One other problem with having a brick-and-mortar location for a spa is that you have to be there all the time in order to make money. Your spa could be completely empty, yet you have to be there waiting and hoping for someone to show up. By making your spa mobile, you don't have to sit around for potentially nothing.

Whenever you have downtime, you get to be at home. You can focus on marketing or you can be relaxing. You're going to book clients for certain time periods, so you don't have to worry about walk-ins or anything like that.

You know when you'll be working and when you won't be because you're creating your own schedule based on when you decide to book people. It's great! With a brick-and-mortar, you have to be open at least 6 days (preferably 7) a week and for most hours during the day.

Not only that but you then have to give massages and serve clients all day which can be exhausting. You're going to get burnt out very quickly if you try to do everything by yourself. If you don't want to run the show by yourself, then you're going to have to hire staff right from the jump to help you out.

With a mobile spa, it's far easier to run the show by yourself when you first get going. Then you can easily scale at your own pace whenever you feel comfortable doing so. You can also continue operating the business by yourself if you want to.

It's a lot easier to avoid burnout when you can focus on servicing your clients more so than having to upkeep a physical store.

## The Pandemic Changed Things

When Covid-19 happened, everything changed. A lot of businesses had to adapt or they wouldn't survive. Some businesses were closed due to shutdowns and weren't able to survive the pandemic unfortunately.

Covid-19 changed things in the spa industry because spas could no longer serve their clients. People had to stay in their homes due to lockdowns. This changed things in many ways.

More jobs became remote and stayed that way. People ordered more delivery. People essentially got more comfortable staying at home than they previously did because of the pandemic.

In regards to the spa industry, someone might not want to go out to go to a spa. They may have more of a preference for having the convenience of someone coming over to their home. A mobile spa is the perfect way to adapt to how things have changed due to the pandemic.

## It's Easier to Make Time for Someone to Come to You

People need to pamper themselves. They need to rest, relax, and destress from their busy and stressful lives. The problem is making time to be able to rest and relax.

It can be more of a challenge to go to a physical location to get the self-care someone needs, as opposed to having someone come directly to you. This means you'll be more likely to get booked because of how much easier it is to fit into someone's schedule.

## The Benefits Outweigh the Cost

You're in the business of making other people feel relaxed. You get to make people feel beautiful or help them destress. That is hard to put a price on.

This is why people are willing to pay good money in order to get a massage or to get pampered. Getting a massage or other spa-related service may not be a necessity like some other things, but the demand is definitely there. If you're able to properly market yourself, you'll have no problem landing clients.

# Chapter 2: What Does It Take to Get Up and Running?

How do you get started with this business? There are different ways you could go about this, but it's important that you think and plan some things before you dive right in. This chapter is going to cover the things you need to consider before you serve your first client.

## What Services Are You Going to Offer?

The very first thing I want you to think about is the types of services you're going to offer. Are you a licensed massage therapist, but you're not a qualified esthetician or nail technician? If so, then you're going to be limited in what you can offer unless you look to implore some outside help right from the jump.

You can cover the massages and you hire an esthetician who can cover other services such as facials or waxing. You could also bring on a nail technician to provide manicures and pedicures. If you want to offer all of these types of services right from the jump and still do everything by yourself in the beginning, then you're going to have to make sure you're licensed to handle any of the services you wish to provide.

If not, what you can offer will be limited in the beginning, which isn't the end of the world. You'll want to expand your offering because chances are good that you'll be missing out on potential business if all you can offer is a massage for example. The best case scenario for a mobile spa is being able to offer massages, facials, and other such esthetician services, as well as manicures and pedicures.

Right off the bat, you'll need to decide if you want to get qualified to handle all of these services, or if you want to hire to cover other services you're not qualified for. If you want to hire soon after you open don't worry, I have more information that will be covered on this matter in a later chapter. Conversely, if you're only a licensed massage therapist or esthetician and you want to increase your qualifications, go ahead and get the business up and running and work on your qualifications as you go.

Only offer what you can in the beginning and then you can expand your offering once you become qualified to do so. Don't wait to start your business if you're already qualified to offer a certain spa-related service.

It can take some time to build up your clientele base, so you don't want to delay starting your business to get pre-qualifications. If you currently don't have any qualifications, then wait until you do because it's not going to do you any good to get a client that you can't serve.

## Establish the Business

Once you decide on the services you're going to offer, the next thing you need to do is officially establish your business. For a mobile spa, your best options are going to be a sole proprietorship or an LLC. You also have to option to set up a corporation, but this likely isn't going to be necessary especially if you're starting out by yourself.

LLC stands for limited liability company and its main job is to offer a barrier between you and your business. It basically separates your personal assets from your business' assets. With a DBA (doing business as) or sole proprietorship, there is no barrier.

The business and yourself are one in the same. So why does this matter? Well if a lawsuit were to happen, people could go after your personal assets because you are your business.

If your business is a completely separate entity, then that isn't the case. If your business is separate from yourself, someone can only go after your business and not your personal belongings. It's up to you to decide how you want to go about things, but that's the main consideration for forming an LLC.

A sole proprietorship is much easier to establish and get started with so there are pros and cons to any entity type that you would consider opening.

## Cover Yourself

Something that I would say isn't up for debate is getting proper insurance for your business. The main two types of insurance you're going to want to look into are going to be general liability insurance and professional liability insurance. General liability insurance is going to help cover general things that may happen with your business.

For example, maybe you get some oil on a piece of the client's furniture. Maybe you damage a wall when bringing in your massage table, or your table breaks or falls over with the client on it and they sustain an injury. These are the kind of scenarios you'll want to have general liability insurance for.

Professional liability insurance is going to help cover claims against things such as malpractice. Maybe a client develops a rash or breaks out in hives from a cream that you used. These are things you need to think about when starting your business, which is why business insurance is so important.

Hopefully nothing like this does happen, but you have to prepare for it just in case. It's better to be prepared rather than to have your business potentially fail due to a lack of proper planning.

## Any Other Licenses?

This is where there's going to be some variance in regard to where you live. You're going to need a state license to operate your business in the state that you live in, but you may also need a city license for each different city that you want to operate in.

The best way to determine what licenses you'll need for your area will be to contact your local county's office to get more information for the area that you live in.

# What About Materials and Supplies?

If you're giving massages, you can do that with your hands, but that's not all there is to it. You're going to need some other things to complete your massage and set a relaxing tone for your service.

The types of supplies you'll need will vary depending on what specific services you decide to offer. Here are some general things you'll likely need to think about:

## Massage Table and/or Facial Bed

You're going to need a way to perform your services so getting a massage table is a must. Some models are adjustable, which is perfect to allow you to be able to perform different services. If you're starting off not offering massages, then a facial bed may be more appropriate.

I recommend getting something that offers you the most versatility, which is going to be an adjustable massage table. A good massage table is going to cost around $200-$300.

## Other Basics

You're also going to need a cart that you can put your supplies in and wheel around easily so that you have everything you need close by. You're also going to need an adjustable chair that you can sit on when you provide your services.

You also want to think about what creams, lotions, waxes, stones, oils, portable pedicure spa, sheets for your table, hot towel warmer, etc that you're going to need for the specific services that you're offering.

## Setting the Tone

You have no idea what you could be walking into when you arrive to serve a client. A client could be living in a home that's unorganized or a little chaotic at times. It can be hard for people to relax if the surroundings around them aren't congruent with a calm environment.

This is where you can help to better set the mood by bringing in some candles or flowers to help better set the mood. If it's Valentine's Day, you could bring rose petals to help set the mood for the occasion. You want to be able to bring a few basic things that can help your client to feel more relaxed regardless of what their current home environment is like.

## A Vehicle

You're going to need a way to get from client to client and the best way to do that is going to be with your own car. Luckily this can be done with your own personal vehicle so long as it has the space for your supplies. One way you can operate this business is by getting a large vehicle, such as a bus, and converting it into a spa.

This way everything is set up in it and you can simply arrive at the client's home and serve one person or multiple people at the same time from your bus. This isn't a bad idea by any means, but it's certainly going to increase the start-up costs needed for this business. If you already have a vehicle that's capable of carrying everything you need, why not start off in a way that's more cost-efficient?

You can serve people in their own homes or outdoor patios if they prefer and skip the cost of buying a large bus. Once you build up your clientele, you can consider the bus route as an option, but don't feel like you need to do this in the beginning.

## The Start-Up Costs Are Good

All things considered, the start-up costs for a mobile spa really aren't that bad. Yes, it can vary quite a bit depending on what services you're offering from the start, but you're saving a ton of money by being mobile and not having to purchase a bus or anything like that. Once you get your basic supplies, it's not going to cost that much to refill the supplies that you do need.

If you are having to refill supplies, that's a good thing because it means you're using them for clients, so you're getting paid. This is why the margins on a mobile business are higher than for a brick-and-mortar spa.

A physical location is going to have a lot more overhead due to paying for the lease, paying for employees, and insurance costs are going to be higher as well. You might have to dip into savings a little bit to get everything you need, but it's nothing unreasonable. Your ongoing expenses are not going to be that high.

# Chapter 3: How to Promote Your Mobile Spa

So you've gotten to the point where you've set up your business and you've gotten the supplies you need to execute your service. What do you do now? Sitting around and waiting for clients to start contacting you is not a good strategy.

You need to be strategic and proactive in your approach to be able to get new clients on board. By the end of this chapter, you'll know how to be efficient with your marketing efforts to bring in new clients consistently.

## Who is Your Ideal Client?

The very first thing you need to understand about marketing is that if you try to appeal to everyone, you will appeal to no one. That might not make sense because wouldn't you want to market to everyone? You don't want to exclude people who might be interested in your services right?

Well, the problem is that when you try to market to everyone, your marketing messages become too generalized. It's not really speaking to any single person. Instead, it's just a very plain and boring message.

It's not going to push anyone to want to book a massage or other such service with you. This is why you need to get very specific with the type of person that you want to serve. For example, let's say you want to target moms in their 30s and 40s who work at a corporate office.

Now with your marketing, you can speak directly to the pain points and other issues this type of person experiences. When someone in your niche sees your marketing material, they'll be much more inclined to say, "Oh that's definitely me!", which is exactly the type of response that you want. If you get someone thinking this, they're going to be far more likely to book an appointment with you.

Yes, you might be eager to start marketing to get your name out there, but I want you to slow down for a second. If you jump right in without knowing who you're targeting, then it's going to be a wasted effort. You're going to be left feeling frustrated for all of your hard effort not leading to any new clients.

## How to Determine Your Ideal Client

There's a multitude of different kinds of people that you could serve. There's not necessarily a better type of person to serve over another, but there are a couple of things you need to consider. First of all, you're opening a mobile spa.

You're likely going to be offering services such as facials, manicures, and pedicures. If you offer these services and only target males, then you're going to have a tough time. Females are predominantly interested in these types of services.

If you're only offering massages, then this could be a different story. However, most spas are going to target women as their main customers. This isn't to say you won't ever have male customers.

You certainly can for couples packages, or a male might be interested in a certain service that you offer. The main thing you want to think about is what you're offering and which type of person would be most interested in these services. The other thing you want to think about is income level.

If you target younger people in their early 20s who just graduated college, they're not going to be as established as someone who's had more time to establish their career. This is why income is also an important thing to think about. You might be targeting women, but if they don't have enough discretionary income for your service, then you could still struggle to be successful.

Imagine if one spa targeted 20-25-year-old men and another targets women in their early 30s to mid-40s. Which spa do you think has a better chance to succeed? It's obviously the one targeting women in their early 30s to mid-40s.

The other company can put in 10 times the amount of effort into marketing and it won't make a difference. They will still fail based solely on who their ideal customer was.

## What Are Your Personal Interests or Experiences?

When trying to narrow down to your ideal customer, it's important to think about yourself. What are your personal interests and experiences? What are previous jobs or careers that you've been a part of?

This is helpful because you can easily think about and relate to the pain points that these people are experiencing. For example, maybe you used to work in a corporate office and you wanted a change of pace where you were out and about more. So you left your corporate office job to open up a mobile spa.

You can totally relate to everything someone might be experiencing in their own corporate office job. You were probably stressed out all the time, your work followed you home, and you didn't have enough time with your kids.

These are things you can talk about with your marketing. You have the insider knowledge because you've personally lived it yourself.

## What if You Can't Relate to Your Target Client?

Let's pretend you're someone who loves sports, but you've never been an athlete yourself. You love the idea of working with athletes and helping them recover with a massage and helping them relax with other services that you offer. Since you haven't played sports yourself, you're having a hard time understanding their exact needs and struggles. How can you overcome this?

This is where it helps if you have someone you know who is in your interested niche. So do you know of someone who is or was an athlete? If so, pick their brain about the hardships and struggles they experienced being an athlete.

If you don't know of any, scour the internet for forums and videos where athletes talk about their experiences. It could be that they don't have any personal time, and getting out to get a massage is simply too time intensive. This is where you can come in and market your mobile services as a way to make it easy to get your massages in even if you're constantly practicing your sport.

## What This Might Look Like

Here's a sample ad to show what something might look like when you do narrow down your niche. In this example, your target niche is women in their early 30s to mid-40s with kids and a stressful corporate job.

"Are you stressed to the max with work? No matter where you go, does it follow you around? Do you barely have any time for yourself once you're finally able to shut your laptop and get the kids to bed? Look I get it, I'm a busy mom myself and I had to find a way to make time for myself.

You deserve to spoil yourself a little bit. Your coworkers and family depend on you to be your best, but how can you if you're not making time for yourself? Book an at-home spa day and let me do all of the heavy lifting for you! It doesn't have to be all day, I can be in and out in an hour if you're crunched for time. Click the link below and do your inner circle a favor by booking an appointment."

Do you see how targeted you can make your marketing material when you really drill down who it is you want to work with? This one thing can absolutely be the difference between success and failure. Make sure you take care of this first before you go and do any actual marketing.

## Get Your Website Going

As of the writing of this book, you need a website. We live in the digital age. People are going to look you up online and see what you're all about. If they can't find your website, that's going to be a red flag to potential customers.

If your website doesn't look professional, then that's going to turn people away as well. You have to have a website and it needs to look high-quality as well. You might not have any experience creating websites and that's likely the case.

If this is the boat you find yourself in, I recommend that you outsource this process and hire someone such as a freelancer who can create the perfect website for your business. Look at other spa websites to get an idea for the types of things that you want to include on your website. You can have a calendar on your website to allow customers to book an appointment themselves, and you can also include your phone number.

This is a good option in case people have specific questions. You can walk them through the process and book them for an appointment once you answer all of their questions. This is the main thing you want to ensure is on your website.

If a client isn't able to get in contact with you or book an appointment themselves, then what's the point? It's also a good idea to include any testimonials you receive from your clients. This is a great way to help build trust with someone who may be on the fence about booking with you.

## Running Advertisements

I want to talk about some strategies you can use to help build up your client base. One thing you can definitely do is pay to get exposure to an entirely new audience who has never heard of you before. Running ads in the digital world is easier now than ever before.

You don't have to pay thousands upon thousands of dollars to advertise on the radio or television. Instead, you can use social media to get directly in front of your target customer. Yes, it is going to cost some money to advertise your business on social media.

Most platforms do allow for budgets as small as $5 per day. This means that for about $150 per month, you can continually put your business in front of new people. No worries if you don't have that kind of money to put towards ads, there are other ways you can market your business for free.

I personally think that ads are great because you can get very targeted with who sees your ad. It's not like it's a bunch of random people who are seeing your ad. So let's say you do want to run a $5-a-day budget on an ad.

How do you know who you should be targeting? Well, it's a good thing you already determined this or at least you should have. If you already determined who your ideal customer is, then you're set.

You can target the age range you want and what their likes and interests are. So if my ideal clients are female soccer players in their late 20s and early 30s, I can specially target females. Then I can target only females who are in their late 20s to early 30s.

Next, I can show my ad to people who have shown an interest in soccer. Now I'm especially targeting my niche. I can also write my ad based on what would speak most to these specific people and that's how you can create a profitable ad.

Compare that to going in blindly. You're targeting anybody and everybody, and your ad copy is generic so people just scroll right past your ad.

That's an easy way to burn through some money quickly, which is not what you want. My guess is that you don't want to waste your money, so you have to be smart with your ad budget.

## Don't Be Afraid to Hustle

Marketing isn't all about advertising. In fact, there are free or close to free ways that you can effectively promote your business. One of the best ways to freely promote your business is to get out in your own community.

What I'm talking about is handing out flyers to promote your business. This may sound a little old school, but it's highly effective if you go about it in the right way. If you just hand out flyers at some random place, it's likely going to be a waste of your time.

If you hand out your flyers to places where your ideal client is, then you can make some headway doing this. I want you to stop and think about the different places your ideal client goes to. If your ideal clientele are moms with young children, then go to daycares and offer to drop off your flyers at the front desk or if a few can be posted on a bulletin board.

Go to local gyms in your area because people who workout could be more likely to take care of themselves with a massage. If your target clients like to shop at natural grocery stores, then you should be going to natural grocery stores looking to leave some of your flyers with them or on a bulletin board.

Is there a local restaurant that people in your town like to go to? Stop by there as well. The more places you drop your flyers off at, the more effective this method will be. You can't drop off some flyers at one location and call it good. You need to try as many different places as you can think of.

## Build Your Online Presence

Not only do you need to focus on going out and about, but you need to promote yourself as much as possible online as well. There are plenty of free platforms out there that allow you to do this, and of course, I'm talking about social media. It doesn't matter who your target customer is, they are on social media and are using it daily.

The problem is that people on social media have short attention spans. You can't post once per week and expect anyone to remember your business. They're going to forget all about what you have to offer in a matter of seconds if you don't do a good job of grabbing their attention.

Even if you do grab their attention, you probably won't have it for long which is why you need to post often. Preferably you need to post once per day on your social media accounts, but only do what you can manage. You don't need to be on every platform, pick one or two that you're familiar with and post regularly on those platforms.

# How to Easily Post More Consistently

There's a lot that goes into making a post online. First, you have to think of what you want to post about. Then you have to write out the post and put a picture with it.

Then you actually have to post it and think of what hashtags you want to use. That's a lot to think about for one post! Imagine having to do this every day, on top of everything else you have going on in your business and personal life.

Posting every day can feel like a never-ending grind and quickly lead you to burnout, especially in a service-based business like the spa industry. You need to use a social media planner that will allow you to plan out and post your social media posts for you. You can simply upload the picture and type out the text ahead of time and tell it to post on Thursday at 7:00 p.m.

Then when 7:00 p.m. on Thursday rolls around, it'll automatically post without you having to do anything. This allows you to work in batches when it comes to your social media content. You can sit down and have a brainstorming session coming up with a bunch of different post ideas.

Then you can write out all of your posts and put them in the planner. You could do this once per week if you want to. So on Mondays, you could write out your content for the entire week through next Monday and put it in your planner.

Now you're only having to make an effort one time per week as opposed to every single day. As for coming up with ideas, this is something you could do less often such as twice per month. Come up with different ideas that you might want to post about soon.

Come up with extra ideas because when it comes time to make a post, you might not like the idea you originally had when you first came up with it. It's a lot easier to come up with new ideas once you get into your creative zone. This is far better than sitting there every day wondering what to post about.

What usually happens is that you fall behind and then you end up not posting as frequently as you should. When that happens, you're missing out on free exposure for your business, so you definitely want to avoid this mistake!

# Could You Give Me a Hand?

Let me help you out a bit to get started. You might not have a clue what kinds of posts you should be making. The good news is that there are so many different things that you could post about that it shouldn't be too hard to come up with some solid ideas.

You definitely want to post videos of you servicing your clients or any type of post that's a customer testimonial. You posting about your job does a couple of things for you. First, it shows that you're staying busy.

This helps to build that social proof. Other people are booking you so I might as well too! If your business looks like a ghost town, people might be hesitant to book because they're wondering why no one else is getting your service.

Posting this type of content also shows you're a professional, and that you're experienced and good at what you do. Finally, it can make other people want to experience the same thing because it looks so relaxing, so they click the link to your website to book an appointment. Also, if people leave a review for you or have nice things to say, you definitely want to spread the word and let your followers know.

People are not going to book an appointment with you if they don't trust you. They need to trust that you're a person who will do a good job and not try to steal from their home. They need to trust that you can do a good job with the services you offer.

People look to what others have experienced to help them make a decision. This is why sharing positive reviews on your social media can be very beneficial for your business.

## Educational Based Content

Another type of content that you can make are posts where you're educating the readers about something related to your niche. For example, you could explain why some people feel sick the day after they get a massage. You could make a post about why someone might feel sore after a massage and what kind of signal the body is telling you.

How often should you get a massage? The benefits the skin receives from getting a facial. The list could go on and on with this type of content.

Educational content helps to show your followers that you're an expert in your given field. This will help to establish you as an authority and help your followers trust you more. It also helps you come up with more content that you can post, and you don't have to worry about educational content hurting your business, especially in this case.

Some people worry that if they teach their followers their best secrets, they won't do business with them. With a mobile spa, people wanted to be spoiled. They want someone else to come in and help them relax.

Plus, it's not like someone can self-massage as well as a professional can massage someone else. Now even if you post about educational content and testimonial content, you still might run out of ideas. Even though this is your business page, you should also post content about who you are as a person.

This might not seem professional, but people are tired of seeing others be fake. People don't want the people they follow to hide behind a mask and act like everything is professional and perfect 100% of the time. They want to see your human side and get to know you better as a person.

Post about whatever you feel comfortable with in regards to your personal life. Maybe you have a cat, so you post funny clips about your cat. You could even make it related to your niche by trying to treat your cat to a spa day, but your cat is just not having it.

Post about what some of your hobbies are. If you like to walk trails in your neighborhood, then post about it.

It really can be anything, so don't overthink it. It's more so about giving yourself more content to post and helping your audience get to know you on a deeper level.

## Target Certain Days During the Year

The cool thing about a spa business is that there are certain times of the year that you can take advantage of. Mother's Day, Valentine's Day, bridal showers, bachelorette parties, etc. These are days or seasons that you really want to take advantage of.

Days like Mother's Day and Valentine's Day can really make or break your business. People want to do something special for their mom and people want to do something special for their significant other. The same goes for wedding season.

Usually, peak wedding season is in the summer months, but if you live in a warmer climate, then your area's peak wedding season might be more in the fall or spring. Regardless, you want to make sure that you have a plan in place to fully take advantage of these specific days or time periods in your business.

Simply making a post the day before Mother's Day about a special you're running isn't going to cut it. If you make a post the day before Mother's Day, then guess what? You're already too late! Most people will have already bought their mom a gift before then.

If someone is looking for a last-minute gift, they might get some flowers and a gift card at the store. This doesn't mean your post about your special will be a complete waste, but you're missing out on everyone who already bought their mom a gift well in advance. You have to be better prepared if you want to maximize your bookings on these special days.

# How to Take Advantage of Valentine's Day

Valentine's Day is an interesting one because you're dealing with couples. So you're going to want to run promotions for couples massages and things of that nature. The interesting part is how you go about marketing it.

If your ideal client is a female, then it's likely that most of your followers on social media are female. You definitely want to make sure that you promote your offer to men as well. Men need to get their partner something, and a massage package is a great gift idea.

However, they're not going to see any post you make on your business profile because they're not following you. This is why you're going to need to advertise your promo on social media to ensure that men see it. You're also going to want to increase your ad spend from what it normally is.

This is a day you really want to maximize to the fullest. By using a combination of organic posts on social media and advertisements, you can make the most of this holiday.

# Taking Advantage of Mother's Day

How you go about handling Mother's Day is going to differ from Valentine's Day. The reason for this is that daughters will already be following your personal social media page. So with this holiday, you can lean more towards organic posts if your marketing budget for ads is a little tight.

However, you'll still want to advertise on social media if possible because husbands and sons will want to get their wife or mom a gift for Mother's Day. You also have to think about your promotion. Should you offer a single massage?

Or should you offer mother-and-daughter spa packages? My advice is that when you're advertising on social media, you should offer a spa package for just the mom.

When you're promoting your offer on your social media pages organically, then you can offer mother and daughter packages in addition to packages for just the mom. You never know, a mom who follows you may very well take it upon herself to buy a spa package for herself.

## How Far Out Should You Start Promoting for These Days?

As I mentioned earlier, making a post the day before these special days simply isn't going to do you much good. You want to start well in advance because you want to catch people who will get a gift early. My best recommendation is to start promoting your special one month in advance and have this go until about midday of Mother's Day.

This might seem a little long or excessive, but you have to consider the different kinds of buyers out there. Some people are going to buy a gift well in advance, other people are going to wait until the last minute.

Other people are going to see your offer and then shop around before they make their final decision. So by promoting in advance, you give people plenty of time to decide on what they want to do.

## Advertising for a Specific Day

Let's say your normal ad budget is $5 per day. The month leading up to a day like Valentine's Day or Mother's Day, you're going to want to increase your ad spend. In this case, you'd want to up this to $15 per day if possible, or triple the amount from what you usually do.

If you don't have the budget to increase your ad spend, then slow it down a month or two leading up to when you want to start promoting for the specific day. Instead of running $5 per day every week of the month, you'd now only run $5 per day two weeks out of the month. This will allow you to save some more money that you can allocate towards these Holiday promotions.

The key here is to ensure that you're running your ad every single day up to the promotion. Here's a sample ad you could run for Mother's Day:

"Did your mother give you the world? Why not give back to her in a special way that can help her relax this Mother's Day? As we all know, our moms can be exhausted even though they never show it. This is why I'm offering a special Mother's Day massage. Click the link below and use the promo code "Mothers' Day" to take advantage of this offer."

Here's a sample ad you could run for Valentine's Day:

"Do you want to do something special for your significant other this Valentine's Day? Why not change things up a bit from the typical flowers and chocolate? Why not get your significant other something that benefits you as well? I'm talking about a couple's massage of course. You don't even have to leave your home as I come to you and melt the stress away. Click the link below and use the promo code "Valentine's Day" to book your appointment now."

## How Often to Post on Your Social Media?

When it comes to promoting your special offer on social media, you're not going to post about your offer every single day. That would get redundant and start to annoy people. You still want to make people aware of your promotion well in advance, but posting about it every single day is unnecessary.

On the other hand, if you post about it too infrequently, then nobody is going to remember your offer and people might not even see it in the first place. The best way to go about things is to make two posts per week about your promotion. So if you start one month in advance, then you're going to make a total of 8 posts about your Holiday promotion.

You can use the same text for the ad that you do for your organic social media post. From there you can simply use different variations when you continue to post about the same type of thing. Here's an example:

"Get a gift that will put your significant other to sleep this Valentine's Day! No, I'm not talking about something boring, I'm talking about a couple's massage! Book now using the promo code "Valentine's Day" to receive a special discount."

## Host a Giveaway for These Holidays

You might be a little hesitant at the idea of doing a free giveaway, but hear me out. Yes, you'll be giving away something for free such as a free massage, couples massage, or spa package, but when done correctly, this can generate big business for you. It can also help to create a lot of engagement on your social media profiles.

Again though, you have to go about things in a smart way. You can't drag the contest on for an entire month. People who don't win need to know with plenty of time in advance so they still have time to get a gift.

Giveaways are effective because you can incentivize people to engage and share your content, which means more eyeballs will get on your posts. So if you want to host a free giveaway for Mother's Day, announce it at the start of the promotion for Mother's Day. If you're going to start a promotion for Mother's Day one month in advance, then go ahead and announce your giveaway from the start to kick things off.

Have the giveaway last for one week to give people the opportunity to sign up and announce the winner or winners at the end of it. The first step to ensuring a successful giveaway is to make the prize good. Put yourself in someone else's shoes.

If you were scrolling along on social media, would the possibility of winning a 15% off coupon really excite you that much? It likely wouldn't and you would continue scrolling. In this spa business, it's easy to create a powerful giveaway.

You can use something along the lines of a free massage like I mentioned earlier. You don't want to give away just one prize though. You can also offer something to the second and third-place winners as well.

For example, first place could win a free couple's massage, daughter-mother-massage, or two free individual massages. Second place could receive one free massage. Third place could receive 50% off of a massage or spa package that you choose.

By offering multiple winners, you'll increase the number of people who participate because it's more likely that they'll win something, thus making it worth their time. Yes, this means you'll be giving away a good amount of money in free massages, but it will pay off. The way that you make the most of things is in how people gain an entry into the contest.

People must like, comment, and share the initial post detailing the giveaway in order to enter the contest. You can also have people gain additional entries for each friend that they tag. For example, you could say that for every 3 friends you tag, you'll gain an extra entry to win the contest.

Imagine the compound effect that this can have. People share the post with their followers and some of that person's followers will be interested and sign up and share the post with their followers. This can continue to happen quite a bit and help generate some good traction for your post.

When you end the contest and no longer allow for new entries, you can simply use an online generator to draw three names. The first name drawn gets the first-place prize.

The second name drawn gets the second-place prize and the third name gets the third prize. Here's a sample post you could use to announce your contest:

"What's better than a couple's massage? How about a free couple's massage! This Valentine's Day, I'm giving away a free couple's massage in addition to other prizes. All you have to do to enter the contest is like this post, comment "Valentine's Day," and share this post to gain your entry. You'll gain an additional entry for every 3 friends that you tag on this post up to a maximum of 5 entries per person. I'll go live next Tuesday at 11:00 A.M. Pacific Time to announce the winners. Best of luck!"

With this type of post, you want to be specific about how people can enter, what people can win, when the contest closes, and when the winners will be announced. This will help to eliminate any potential confusion that a reader may have in regards to your contest. It's also a good idea to make a couple of posts reminding people that the giveaway is closing soon to help give people that extra push to join.

## What About Bridal Showers?

Taking advantage of bridal showers and bachelorette parties during peak wedding season is a must as well. It is different from a specific holiday because it lasts longer than just a day. It's not going to make sense to continually blast your followers with a special promo you're running for brides.

However, you still need to do something to make the most of peak wedding season. The first thing you want to do is offer a promo. You can offer a promo that lasts for a week up to 2 different times during peak wedding season.

You don't want to have promos on a regular basis because you'll condition your followers to wait for you to have a sale. Your promo could be something such as 15% off when a group of 5 or more books with you. You could increase or decrease the discount based on the amount of people that partake in the offer.

For instance, you could do 20% off when 8 or more book with you as part of your promo. This way, bridal parties that are big or small can take advantage of your offer. As for posting organically on your social media, you can make a couple of posts about your promo. If your promo lasts a week, posting about it two different times is a good balance and won't annoy anyone.

# Chapter 4: Collecting Payment and Determining Your Rate

Having everything set up and knowing how to market your business is great, but it really doesn't matter if you don't know what to charge. Additionally, you need to think about how you're going to collect payment. These are the types of things you're going to discover in this chapter.

## How Should You Charge?

With a mobile spa, there are a lot of different services that you could potentially offer. You have waxing, facials, manicures, pedicures, and massages just to name a few. With all of these different services, it can be tricky to determine a price for each one and charge a certain amount.

This is why it's typically easier to charge by the hour. You can then assign blocks of time based on how long you think a service will take. For instance, let's say someone wants their eyebrows waxed and that takes you on average 15 minutes.

This means the person could still receive 45 minutes worth of another service to complete the hour. So that might be a 45-minute massage and a 15-minute eyebrow wax. It could just be an hour-long massage, or it could be two different services that each last for 30 minutes to complete the hour.

Charging a flat hourly rate makes things super easy to book and fulfill. If you charge by the service, then you could be wasting a lot of time if the customer asks a bunch of questions or is just talkative in general. If a normal eyebrow wax takes you 15 minutes but it took you 30 because the customer kept talking to you and didn't allow you to get started, well then that's a waste of your time.

You could very well be on a time crunch and be late to your next appointment. If you charge by the hour and know how many hours you'll be there, you avoid all of these problems. Now you know their session is up at 3:00, not whenever you finish the waxing or whatever the service is.

## What's the Minimum?

You might want to consider adding in a minimum number of hours to make things worth your time. Every time you go and service a client, you're having to spend your gas to get there. If the person only wants one quick service that takes 15 minutes, that's not going to be profitable for you.

If you require an hour minimum, you can avoid this headache. How big or small you want your minimum is entirely up to your discretion. At an absolute minimum, you should require someone to book you for at least one hour of your time.

You may want to increase that to at least 2 or even 3 hours, but this is something you can get a better feel for as time goes on. Initially, you don't want to deter people because they're intimidated by the 3-hour minimum. You can consider that once you're more established, but I'd avoid it in the beginning.

When you don't have a lot of clients to begin with, you want to do what you can to help accommodate the customer. Requiring a one-hour minimum is going to be understandable to your customers and it won't deter them from booking with you.

## What Should Your Hourly Rate Be?

How much experience do you have with the spa services that you're offering? How long have you been in business for? How many reviews does your company have?

What are your competitors charging? These are some of the things that will influence what your hourly rate ends up being. On one side of the scale, you could charge a dollar per minute or $60 per hour. In the middle of the road, you could be charging around $100 per hour.

On the high end of things, you could be charging around $150 per hour. It's easy to see that there's quite a large gap between the low end of the scale and the high end of the scale. What I want you to do to determine your specific hourly rate is think about those factors that I mentioned at the start of this section.

## How Much Experience Do I Have?

If you're brand new to being an esthetician, nail tech, or massage therapist, then you simply don't have your skills honed in all the way quite yet. It's going to be really hard to justify a higher price point. Put yourself in the shoes of someone who wants to order a mobile spa package.

Imagine paying a premium price and receiving a service that wasn't bad by any means, but it felt average. You might feel compelled to leave a 3-star review or something along those lines.

Consider the service being exactly the same, but now you paid less for it.

You're happy with the service because the expectations are more in line with what the price for the service was. It can take years and years to truly reach the top 10% in your field for providing these specific services. If your skill level can't back up the price you're charging, then you need to lower your prices.

You're putting yourself in a position to fail because customer expectations are not going to be aligned with what they're being charged.

## How Long Have You Been in Business For?

You could have 5 years of experience working for someone else's spa. That's a lot of good experience, and you definitely know what you're doing when providing your spa services. The problem here is that you're brand new to being in business.

Your business is not established yet. You don't have many reviews. Your social media pages don't have a lot of followers or engagement.

People in your area don't know who you are yet. People aren't sure if they can trust you yet. You might want to charge a high hourly rate. This makes sense when it comes to your skill level.

The level of service you'll be able to provide will be in line with a higher price. The problem is getting customers to book with you. They don't know about your previous work history.

Even if you tell them, they don't know you, so why would they believe you? They're going to compare your high price and lack of reviews against someone else's company that's charging a lot but has the online presence to back it up. You'll have a hard time competing.

If your price point is lower, then you'll give people a reason to choose you even though your business isn't as established yet. You can also charge more than someone who just got licensed and is just setting up their business, but you'll need to charge less than someone whose business is established and has years of experience.

## What Are Others Doing?

As humans, it's natural to look at others to see how to do something. While it would be great if you're the only spa and mobile spa in your area, that likely isn't going to be the case. There are going to be other spas in your area that you're going to have to compete with.

You want to make sure that your price point makes sense in regards to what your competition is charging. If established spa owners in your area charge $120 an hour, it's not going to make sense to charge more than that if people in your area can't afford or simply aren't willing to pay more than $120 an hour.

The state and city you live in greatly affect what people are willing to pay for a spa. In some cities, your price would definitely be higher than in others even though you'd be providing the same spa packages. This is why it's a good idea to do some research on spas in your area to get an idea of what they're charging.

It could be that you live in a rural area and there isn't a mobile spa in your particular town. You could choose to service other small neighboring towns, but it's going to be harder to get a gauge for what you should charge. If this is the scenario you find yourself in, start with a price point on the lower end of the scale I mentioned earlier.

This way if you struggle to consistently book clients, you won't have to wonder if price is the issue. You'll know it's related to something else, such as your marketing or demand might be a little low in your area.

## Putting It Together

Once you take all of these factors into consideration, you should have a good idea as to where your business should be on the pay scale. If you have any doubts, I recommend going lower as opposed to higher. Start somewhere in the range of $60-$80 per hour if you're not sure.

The good news is that you can adjust your price point later on. If you decide to charge $70 per hour, then you're not married to that price point.

Once the phone is ringing off the hook with people who want to book spa packages with you, you can then consider increasing your prices. You'll know when you need to bump up prices when you feel like you need a spa day to recover from all of the work that you're doing!

## Offer Incentives for Groups

Another factor you need to consider for your pricing is offering discounts when people sign up in groups. I briefly talked about this in the marketing chapter with bridal showers, and it's a good idea to consider in general. It's a good way to incentivize people to bring an extra person along for the sake of an extra discount.

You could offer a 5% discount from your normal rate for couples who sign up for a spa package. So if your normal rate is $100 per hour per person, you would charge $95 per person per hour. You can also manipulate the minimum number of hours as well.

You could require that couples book for a minimum of 2 hours when maybe your normal minimum is just one hour. The same premise applies for larger groups. The more people who book together as a group, the larger the discount is.

And you can increase the hour minimum to something like 3 hours for example. The reason why you want to do this is to help offset your expenses. If you're serving a group of 8 people, you're going to have to enlist some outside.

This labor isn't going to be free, so it's going to eat into your profit. If you only work on a group of 8 for an hour, that's hardly worth your time. By increasing the hour minimum, you ensure that you're going to receive enough money to make it worth bringing in the extra help and fulfilling the service.

## Buy in Bulk

You want to have some way to get repeat customers for your business. Repeat business is huge in the spa world. These are people who already used your service and liked it, and they know you're a trustworthy business owner.

Why not give them a little incentive to help them become a repeat customer? Offer them a package where they can buy 2, 5, or 10 massages upfront or whatever type of spa package you want to offer. The more they buy upfront, the bigger the discount is per session.

You could offer 5% off for two massages, 15% off of 5, and 25% off of 10. So if your normal rate is $100 an hour, that would typically cost $1,000 for 10 hours of service. The person can buy 10 upfront for $750 with this special offer.

This is a great idea because it gives you cash upfront. There's no guarantee that the person will fulfill all of their sessions. Regardless, it ensures that person is spending their money with you. It's far better than someone saying they'll reach out to you to book again.

Why not go ahead and get the money while you can? When is the best time to push this offer? It's right after you finish with them!

They're super relaxed and just experienced an amazing spa service with you. Of course, they're going to want more! You have to strike while the iron is hot.

If you wait, they'll start to forget just how relaxed you made them feel. You're not just in the spa industry, you're also in the sales industry, so don't be afraid to push an offer that will benefit the customer. You don't have to get all weird with it either.

At the end of your service, simply ask the customer if there's anything else they need from you. Once they say no, you can say something along these lines:

"Okay great, well I really enjoyed servicing you today. Just so you know I do offer discounts for packages when you buy in bulk. Would you be interested in learning more about this?"

If the customer says yes, this is where you can go into pitching them about your different packages and go for the sign-up right then and there if they're interested in your offer. You might feel a little uncomfortable doing this in which case you can take a more backseat approach after asking if they need anything else from you:

"Awesome, I'm glad you liked the spa treatment this morning. I actually offer discounts for my spa packages when you buy multiple sessions upfront. I'm going to leave you with this flier that has more information about this offer. You can give me a call for more information or if you're interested in signing up."

This is less of a pushy way to get your point across. The good thing about it is that if someone is interested, they may very well start to ask you questions about it, at which point you can answer their questions and possibly sign them up on the spot anyways. No matter which way you want to go about things, this is something you want to offer to every customer you interact with.

# Chapter 5: Servicing Your Clients

In this chapter, my aim is to give you some tips and considerations for how you go about actually servicing your clients. You may already have a lot of knowledge about working in a spa, but there may be some things you haven't thought about when it comes to serving the client in a mobile spa.

## Lay the Foundation

Your work for executing a good service for a client begins before you even show up at their home. You need to ensure that you'll be able to successfully complete an appointment in their home. For instance, the residence could be cluttered, or there could simply not be enough space for you to fold out your massage table or other necessary supplies.

If you just book someone and then go in blindly, you have no idea what you're walking yourself into. It can certainly cause anxiety just thinking about what their home will look like and hoping there's enough space for you to operate. This is something you need to clarify during your booking process.

Ask them where they want the massage or spa service to take place. If they're getting a massage and they live in a nice climate area, they very well may want the massage completed in the backyard. You need to ensure they have some sort of patio that you can set your supplies on.

If not, then check with the client about setting up on grass because your table could damage the grass. You also have to think about if it just rained. If there's mud, your table is going to sink into the mud and get dirty.

Also, think about operating on a flat surface. You don't want to operate on uneven ground or a slope. These are all things you have to think about if the person wants the service performed outside but they don't have a backyard patio.

If the customer wants the service performed indoors, then you need to ask if space allows for it. Explain to them the size of your massage table. Give them dimensions and a comparison.

For instance, you could say that your massage table is 75" in length and about 35" in width or about the size of a twin mattress. You then would ask the customer if they have space to accommodate the table but also extra space around it for your cart so that you have room to operate. Sometimes though, it can be hard for a customer to gauge exactly how much space you need and if they have enough room.

This is where it can be helpful to do a quick video call with the customer so that they can show you the layout of their home. You'll be able to get a good grasp on how much free space is available for you to use. You may not be able to do this with every customer, but it's worth doing when possible.

Also, inform the customer that any clutter in the room will need to be picked up so that you can freely move around. You won't be able to help the client clean up the house, and if the appointment starts at 11, then that's when the customer starts getting charged. It doesn't matter if they have to spend the first 15 minutes tidying up the room.

If you communicated this in advance during the booking process, then this shouldn't be an issue. Granted these potential issues can be avoided by operating from your own bus, but that can be expensive. Until you get to that point, take the extra precautions ahead of time to ensure that things go smoothly when you arrive.

## Expectations on When the Clock Starts

Another thing you want to go over with the customer is how they'll be charged. Since they're being charged by the hour, you need to set clear boundaries for when the service starts and when it ends. For example, let's say someone books you for an hour-long massage from 1:00 until 2:00.

Make it clear that you'll need to arrive to the residence at 12:30 to set up and ensure that things are ready to go at 1:00. Then once 1:00 hits, the clock starts. The clock starts at 1:00 regardless of what's going on with the customer.

Let's pretend the customer is out running errands and doesn't make it back home until 12:55. This means you won't get to start setting up until 12:55, and for the sake of this example let's say it takes you 15 minutes to get everything set up and ready to go. In this case, the service isn't starting until 1:10, but the customer's hour already started 10 minutes ago.

They'll essentially get a 50-minute session instead of an hour long. This may not seem fair, but again communication is the key here. You communicated that the customer needed to be home 30 minutes before the appointment started so the expectations were clear.

It isn't your fault that they showed up late. This is also part of the reason why you tell them that you're showing up 30 minutes ahead of time. It creates more leeway for the customer because if they are finishing up errands, they'll hopefully hurry up to get home in time for that 30-minute window.

Even if they're a bit late, you still have some time to set up before the appointment actually starts. If you tell the customer you'll be there 10 minutes ahead of time, the customer has a smaller window to be late before it eats into their appointment time.

## Show Up on Time and Have a Good Attitude

How awkward would it be if you told the customer that you would be arriving 30 minutes early only to show up right before the appointment starts? What if their appointment is at 2:00, but you show up late so you don't finish setting up until 2:10? At that point, it's only right to go until 3:10, and if you're unable to because of your schedule, then the customer only needs to be charged for 50 minutes and not an hour.

Showing up late is an incredibly bad look to the customer. It makes you look hypocritical if you say you're going to arrive 30 minutes early. It makes customers have doubts.

If you're unprofessional with how you show up, how will the service be? It can lead to bad reviews as well. You also want to make sure you have a great attitude at all times.

This can be hard to do because the work is exhausting. However, the last thing you want is for the customer to think that you're in a bad mood. Put yourself in the customer's shoes. Picture yourself getting a massage to help yourself relax, but something seems off with the massage therapist.

They're being a little short with you and their facial expressions seem bland. Are you going to be able to fully enjoy the massage? Or are you going to be thinking about the mood the therapist is in the entire time?

Even if the massage is great, it could still be the difference between you giving the therapist a 3-star rating as opposed to a 4 or 5-star rating, so why leave it to chance?

## Use Towels and Belt Holsters

When you're operating a mobile spa, you're going to be dealing with a lot of products such as oils, creams, lotions, and other things of that nature. You want to ensure that you take extra precaution to not get any oil or anything like that on the customer's furniture or other belongings. For example, you wouldn't want to place an oil directly on a furniture surface that the customer owns.

You could very easily get oil droplets on the furniture and damage it. Make sure that you use towels to place any products on to ensure a barrier between your products and the surface they're on. This is also where something like a cart or belt holster comes in handy.

A belt holster will allow you to keep all of your necessary products on yourself for when they're needed. You can also use a cart to keep supplies on as well. As long as you think about the environment you're in and ease with caution with the products you're using, you shouldn't have anything to worry about.

# Chapter 6: More Than Just Me, Prepping for Your First Hire

If you want this business to be just yourself, you can totally do that. You need to be aware that this will limit your service though. You won't be able to offer any couple's packages or packages for bigger groups of people such as bridal showers.

This can severely hurt your business over the years. If you're brand new, don't feel like you need to go out and find people to hire right away. It's a good idea to get your feet wet in the business first.

Get your first clients and service them. Figure out your systems and processes and what works best for you. If you dive right into trying to hire people without doing that first, how will you know how to train them?

How will you know if you like their way of doing things over what your processes could be? You're already starting behind the 8 ball because once someone comes in and gets used to operating a certain way under you, it's going to be hard for them to change their ways.

In this chapter, you're going to learn when you need to start the hiring process and what to look for when choosing the correct candidates for your business. There are quite a few mistakes you can make when choosing to hire someone, and just one wrong hire can severely hurt your business.

## Should You Hire? If so, When?

Typically, when it comes to service-based businesses, you can operate the business entirely by yourself if you wanted to. For example, let's say you open a hair salon. You could operate by yourself and cut people's hair being the only person in your business.

The other option you have is to hire more stylists so that you can service more people overall. This is how things typically work in a service-based business. You can go to a certain point until you're capped at which point you'd need to bring in extra help to continue to service more people.

With a spa business, things are different because right off the bat you need other people to help you out so that way you can offer certain packages for couples and bigger parties. As a hairstylist, there's no reason that two or more people need to get their haircut at the same time. Therefore you could operate solely by yourself if you wanted to.

So when should you start looking to bring on some extra help for couples, bigger parties, or just to serve more clients in general? You want to start looking pretty soon after you feel comfortable with the systems and processes in your business. Once you feel like you have your operations down pat, go ahead and start looking for quality candidates who can help you out.

If you don't do this, then you're going to be missing out on huge revenue potential. You won't be able to offer any sort of special promotions on Valentine's Day because you won't be able to serve two people at the same time by yourself. You won't be able to market to brides during wedding season.

You'll miss out on this year after year because you weren't willing to take that leap. Yes, it can be scary to think about having to pick the right candidate. It can be scary to think about having to pay someone else, but don't worry, this chapter will be a great guide to help put your mind at ease.

## Contractor vs Employee

Before we get into some good hiring practices, I need to make something clear. You're not looking to hire anyone as an employee for your business. An employee will expect regular hours and there are other things such as providing sick leave, paid time off, and insurance.

These are all very normal things someone will expect to have as an employee of a company. Providing regular work hours such as 20, 30, or even 40 hours per week to someone would be tough on you. You'd essentially be in a pickle.

You need to build your business with the help of others, but you likely won't have enough jobs to justify consistent hours for someone. How would you be able to afford consistently paying someone if the business isn't getting consistent jobs yet? You really wouldn't be able to, so you'd have to delay hiring anyone, which means you can only service one person at a time, thus keeping your business small.

The way you get out of this problem is by hiring people as contractors. This means you'll only be working with these people on an as needed basis. There's no expectation for consistent hours, PTO, or anything of that nature.

Yes, they're still representing your company, so you want to hire professionals, but they're not employed by you. They're working for you as an independent contractor. They complete the job, you pay them for the job and the deal is done until the next job pops up.

The good thing about a contractor is that they're only getting paid if you're getting paid. You don't have to worry about paying someone for nothing if you don't have any jobs.

You don't have to worry about not having the money to pay your contractors. You'll have the money because if your contractor is being used, it's because you have jobs going on.

## Where to Find Your First Hire?

When you're ready to make your first hire, where should you look? There are a lot of different places that you could look to, so where should you start? I first recommend looking in your network from people you may have met over the years in the spa industry.

Do you know of anyone who was in your class to get licensed as an esthetician or massage therapist? Did you previously work at a spa with someone else who might be interested in helping you out? This is going to be the best place to look because these are people who already have the qualifications you're looking for.

You also already know these people, or at the very least know a little about them if you had a class together. There are two aspects that must be covered for a good hire. The first is that the person is qualified with the proper licenses and that they are actually good at providing the service or services you need from them.

The second thing is that they are a professional. They practice good hygiene, show up on time, and have a great attitude when interacting with clients. By looking to your inner circle first, you'll know if both of these aspects are covered by anyone you'd potentially be interested in hiring.

## Online Groups

Using online groups can be a great way to source for potential candidates. You can join groups based on various spa-related things such as massage groups, esthetician groups, general spa groups, etc. These groups are going to be filled with people who are interested in getting a certain license or who have already gotten their license.

Ideally, you'll want to join groups that are based on the area that you live in. This way when you post about a job opening, everyone who is interested can be a potential candidate. If you live in Washington State and someone from New York sees your opening, it's not going to do much good unless the person is willing to relocate, which is unlikely.

The key with this is to be involved with these groups. If you join and immediately post about your job opportunity, it can come across as spammy and deter people from taking an interest in what you have to offer. Be an involved member of the groups that you join by making posts and commenting on other group members' posts.

You should do this soon after you start your business. This way when it comes time to post about a job opening, you'll already be well-known and liked in these various groups. Don't assume that you're wasting your time in groups with people who are already massage therapists, nail technicians, or whatever else.

You don't know what their situation is. They may be employed by another company, but they might be looking to get some extra hours on the side. They might want a change of pace or to get away from a bad boss.

They could be running their own business, but they're struggling to get consistent leads, so they could need some extra hours working for someone else. There are a lot of possibilities, so don't assume anything until you try it out and see how it works.

## Online Job Posting

Once you've exhausted both of the above options, you may or may not have found any quality candidates that you're looking for. At this point in your search, you need to start using an online platform that can help bring candidates to you that you can sort through. Yes paying to post a job listing on an online job board isn't going to be free, but it will bring in a lot of candidates.

It's going to take some time to sift through all of the applications, but it's time well invested. Sure, some of the candidates aren't going to have the proper qualifications, but you should get some good people applying for your job. Keep in mind you don't know anything about these people.

You know people in your network and you can build a relationship with people in online groups over time. With a job board, you're not going to know anyone who applies. You can only base your decision on who to interview based on what their resume looks like.

Most importantly, they must have the qualifications you're looking for. They must be licensed to provide the services you need them to. It doesn't matter how everything else looks on their resume.

Next, you want to see how much experience they have working as a massage therapist, esthetician, etc. You need to determine how much work experience you want candidates to have to be considered for the job. A typical standard is at least one year of work experience in the field.

You don't want to set the bar high with something like 5 years of experience. You won't have anyone applying for the job because they won't be qualified. Going with someone who's fresh and just got licensed could be a risk because they haven't had the chance to actually work in the field and get real experience to help hone in their skills.

One year of experience strikes a good balance. You'll still have plenty of people who are qualified to apply to the job, and they have a good amount of experience under their belt for when they start working for you.

## Use Your First Hire's Network

As a side note, once you do make your first hire, you can use their network to help potentially find a good candidate for your second hire. I've been at jobs before where this happens. The manager will ask every employee if they know of anyone who would be a good fit for a certain position that they're hiring.

This tends to work out if you do get a suggestion. The reason is because you already know and trust the person currently working for you. They're likely going to associate themselves with other people who are professionals like they are.

They're also not likely to mention someone if they think they'd be a bad fit. If they give a bad reference and the person is unreliable, then it will reflect poorly on them. You can continue to ask for referrals from any of your current workers any time you're looking to bring on another person.

## The Interview Process

Once you come across some candidates you think can be a good fit for your company, it's time to start interviewing candidates. The best way to conduct an interview is going to be over a video call. You're not going to have a physical office that people can show up to and it's not necessary to temporarily rent a space for a day to conduct interviews.

Conducting interviews over a video call will give you plenty of info to know who you should hire and who you should stay away from. Firstly, make sure they are on time for the video call. If someone can't even show up on time for a video call, then what are the chances they'll be able to show up on time for appointments?

Secondly, pay attention to how they're dressed. Yes, you'll only be able to see the upper half, but that still matters. You don't want someone looking like they rolled straight out of bed and are in their pajamas.

You still want them to dress professionally and like they actually care about getting the job. Here are some questions you can ask during the interview:

"If they're currently employed: Why are you leaving your current role?"

"If they're currently unemployed: What happened at your previous role?"
"What is your biggest strength?"
"What is your biggest weakness?"
"Describe a conflict you had with a customer and how you overcame it."
"Do you work better alone or with a team?"
"Describe a time where you had a conflict with your manager and how you overcame it."
"How would your previous employer describe you?"
"Do you have professional and general liability insurance?"

Some of these questions are going to be particularly important. For instance, you want someone to answer and say that they work well alone and with a team. The reason is they're going to be working alone sometimes and they're going to work as a team sometimes as well.

If they don't get along well with others, it's going to limit the opportunities you're able to give this person. Asking them to describe how they resolved a conflict with a customer is important as well. You want to see how they're able to solve problems on the job.

Do they handle conflict in a professional manner? Do they try to resolve things on their own when they should reach out to you for guidance? These are things you want to look for when a candidate is answering this question.

With some of the other questions such as "how a previous employer would describe you and resolving conflict with a manager," these questions are meant to gauge how difficult of a time you might have working with this person. If someone had a conflict with a previous manager and they put all of the blame on the manager for the conflict, this could show that this person doesn't take responsibility for issues at the workplace.

There are two sides to every story, but you at least want someone who is proactive in resolving issues as opposed to pointing fingers and playing the blame game.

## The Next Steps

If the interview goes well with a candidate, there are a few more steps you need to take before you bring them on board. The first is to get a practice massage or other service from the person. This will allow you to test their skill set in action rather than just seeing their paper experience.

If that goes well, go out to a couple of jobs with the person and shadow them. You'll want to pay them for the jobs just like you normally would, but you want to see how they interact with the customer. Is everything done the way you'd like?

Are they professional? If everything goes well, you can officially extend them the offer to work for you. And don't be afraid to hire multiple people if there are multiple candidates that you like.

You're going to need people with different specialties and you're going to need more than one extra person to help you out with bigger groups. Patience is the key though, don't rush and feel like you have to hire someone if they aren't going to be a good fit. If you bring on multiple people and are trying to decide on how to divvy out jobs amongst your workers, the best way is to simply rotate between them on every job.

Let's say you have 3 contractors; person A, person B, and person C. The first job goes to person A, the next job you get goes to person B, the third job goes to person C, the fourth to person A, etc.

Let's say the fifth job is a couples massage and requires two people. You'd send out person B and C and then give the sixth job to person A.

## Conclusion

Pampering people and making them feel relaxed is a special feeling. It certainly is better than sitting at a desk all day. By starting your very own mobile spa you get to do work that you enjoy and create your own opportunities.

Being in the service industry isn't always a piece of cake, however, the reward you'll get for your effort is well worth it. Dream big with your business because the opportunity is certainly there!